"Lifting belly is so kind. . . . Lifting belly is no joke. . . . Lifting belly is so strong and willing. . . . Lifting belly is so soothing. . . . Lifting belly is so satisfying. . . . Lifting belly is so sweet. . . . Lifting Belly is smooth. . . . Lifting belly is so warm. . . . Lifting Belly is so exciting. . . . Lifting Belly oh lifting belly in time. . . . Lifting belly is astonishing. . . . Lifting belly my queen. . . . Lifting Belly is a miracle. . . . Lifting belly is a language. . . . Lifting belly is here."

Lifting belly is a radical story about lesbian sexuality, about writing about lesbian love making and about loving writing about lesbian sexuality and about loving while writing on lesbian sexuality and about Alice and about Gertrude and about Gertrude loving Alice while writing Lifting Belly, and about Alice loving Gertrude and about ways of being a loving one and about you and about me and about our loving and about kissing and about kissing with a fire and about . . . "Oh dear I said. I was tender, fierce and tender."

When Gertrude Stein writes "Eclair," she asks us "Is it clear?" and she also tells us about the pastry eclair, a pastry with two pieces of pastry and cream in the middle. Is it clear? She asks us to think about this.

Lifting belly say can you see the caesars.
I can see what I kiss.

Can we see Caesar, the nickname for Gertrude Stein? Can we, as she asks in this poem, "read her print?" Can we embrace the gift Gertrude Stein has left us? Can we see the Caesars, the seizures, the muscle spasms, the orgasms? We can see what we kiss. We can read Stein's print because she is writing our own sexuality. We can read her print because we are kissing her, — "When this you see you will kiss me" — because we have kissed each other.

"What did I say, that I was a great poet, like the English, only sweeter."

Lifting Belly

GERTRUDE STEIN

Rebecca Mark, Ed.

Lifting Belly

GERTRUDE STEIN

Rebecca Mark, Ed.

The Naiad Press, Inc.
1989

LIFTING BELLY first appeared in BEE TIME VINE
AND OTHER PIECES (1913–1927) copyright © 1953 by
Alice B. Toklas and in THE YALE GERTRUDE STEIN,
Yale University Press, 1980, and is reprinted with
permission.

The jacket photograph of Alice B. Toklas and Gertrude
Stein is reprinted with permission from the Yale
Collection of American Literature, Beinecke Rare Book
and Manuscript Library, Yale University.

Printed in the United States of America
First Naiad Press Edition 1989

Cover design by Pat Tong and Bonnie Liss
    (Phoenix Graphics)
Typeset by Sandi Stancil

Library of Congress Cataloging-in-Publication Data

Stein, Gertrude, 1874–1946.
    Lifting belly / by Gertrude Stein.
        p.   cm.
    1. Erotic poetry, American. I. Title.
PS3537.T323L5   1989
811.52—dc20   89-34013
                                                CIP

ISBN 0-941483-53-3 : $14.95
ISBN 0-941483-51-7 : $8.95

About the Editor

Rebecca Mark is a writer and teacher who is moving from St. Olaf College in Minnesota to Tulane University in New Orleans where she will teach American Literature, Southern Literature and Feminist Criticism. She is presently writing a book on Eudora Welty's *The Golden Apples*.

Acknowledgments

I would like to thank Joann Loulan for helping me find the voice to write about lesbian sexuality, my friends Mary Wood and Julie Raiskin for brainstorming with me on the talk which led to this edition, Nanc Allen and Jeff Evans for their journey to the Yale Bienecke Library in search of the picture for the back cover, and Mary Ann Brown, Maria Damon and Diane Elliot for their wonderfully helpful comments on drafts of the introduction.

I like loving. I like mostly all the ways anyone can have of having loving feeling in them. Slowly it has come to be in me that any way of being a loving one is interesting and not unpleasant to me.

—Gertrude Stein,
(*The Making of Americans*, 606)

INTRODUCTION

Gertrude Stein is a loving one and the book you have just picked up is a loving book. Slowly as you will read, it will come to you a loving feeling. This is a book to love. When I read *Lifting Belly* in *The Yale Gertrude Stein*, I was so excited that I told everyone I knew about this erotic, lesbian poem. But when I discovered that few of my lesbian friends had ever heard of *Lifting Belly*, I realized that only Stein scholars knew where to find this poem. With the publication of this edition, lesbians will be able to read what many critics have called a lesbian classic, and Stein and *Lifting Belly* will find an audience of women who love women.

Every time I read this poem, I wonder how words which rarely mention a body part can make me feel so aroused. At first, like a new lover, I had no idea what I was reading. Gradually I began to hear Alice and Gertrude making love, talking to each other, talking to the writing itself, speaking to me in a deeply personal, sensuous language. I still had no idea exactly what I was reading, but I began to hear clues.

Not only did I find the rhythm of the language erotic, but I began to hear a story in the music.

Stein wrote *Lifting Belly* between 1915 and 1917, a time of change in her life and all over the world. By 1913 modernism had exploded upon the art, music, and dance scene, changing these artistic expressions forever. In 1913 the Armory show opened in New York, introducing Fauvism and Cubism to America. Matisse was painting. Picasso was painting. Braque was painting. O'Keefe was painting. In 1913 Isadora Duncan was dancing, proclaiming the beauty and power of the uncorsetted female body. In 1913 the Suffragists were fighting for the right to vote. In 1913, the Parisian audience attending Stravinsky's *Le Sacre du Printemps* nearly tore down the house. By 1913, Albert Einstein had established his theory of relativity. In 1913 Gertrude Stein was writing.

Q.E.D., one of the first books Stein wrote, explores a love triangle involving Adele, Helen and Mabel. The real life affair, which lasted from 1901–1903 while Gertrude was in Johns Hopkins Medical School, was a painful experience: Gertrude (Adele) could not fully express her love for May Bookstaver (Helen) because she remained financially and emotionally dependent on Mable Haynes (Mabel). In *Q.E.D.* Stein does not write "about" lesbianism. In *Q.E.D.* Stein does not apologize "for" lesbianism. Instead she writes a book which explores all the ways anyone can have of having loving feeling. *Q.E.D.* is a psychologically sophisticated journey into human loving. But, perhaps because she knew that no one would publish such an honest portrayal of lesbianism,

Gertrude buried this novel for many years. In fact, Gertrude did not live to see any of her openly lesbian works in print.

Instead of writing directly about her own life, she continued her exploration of character in *The Making of Americans: Being a History of a Family's Progress*:

> I write for myself and strangers. No one who knows me can like it. At least they mostly do not like it that everyone is of a kind of men and women and I see it. I love it and I write it. (*The Making of Americans*, 291)

They mostly did not like it. Not until 1912 when Alfred Stieglitz included Stein's portraits of Picasso and Matisse in *Camera Work* and Mabel Dodge published three hundred copies of "Portrait of Mable Dodge at the Villa Curonia," did Stein begin to have a following. During this period she wrote *Three Lives* about a servant woman, Good Anna, a black woman, Melanctha, and a German woman, Gentle Lena, and *Tender Buttons*, experimental poems on "Objects," "Food" and "Rooms." She wrote about lives that had been left out of literature. She wrote in radical new forms. She loved it and she wrote it. And they mostly did not like it.

Her brother Leo Stein thought her work was madness and his dismissal of her talents led to a permanent break in their relationship. In a letter to Mabel Weeks in February, 1913, Leo, who had been Gertrude's closest friend and confidant, wrote: "Gertrude's artistic capacity is I think extremely small . . . Gertrude's mind is about as little nimble as a mind can be" (*Everybody Who Was Anybody*, 101).

Gertrude was deeply hurt but undaunted by these responses. In hopes of finding an audience, she paid to have *Three Lives* published by Grafton, a small American publishing company. The editor wrote a now famous response: "My proof readers report that there are some pretty bad slips in grammar, probably caused in the type-writing" (*Everybody Who Was Anybody*, 83). Gertrude did not allow the editors at Grafton to change a word.

In 1907 Alice B. Toklas sailed to Europe with Harriet Levy. In 1907 Gertrude met Alice B. Toklas. Alice was thirty-one. Gertrude was thirty-three. Alice began to visit Gertrude at 27 rue de Fleurus regularly and to help her type the manuscript of *The Making of Americans*. When Alice's close friend Harriet Levy returned to the United States, Alice moved in with Leo and Gertrude. In 1907 Alice began to listen, to type, and to respond to Gertrude's writing. In 1907 Gertrude's life changed forever. For thirty nine years they loved. For thirty nine years they knew all ways of being loving ones.

In 1914, John Lane, an English publisher, agreed to publish *Three Lives* and Gertrude received her first contract. Soon after this, an American firm, Claire Marie, published *Tender Buttons*. Although critics ridiculed and parodied this radical new work, they began to take note of this American writer living in Paris. In 1914 Leo moved out of 27 rue de Fleurus and, as Gertrude writes in *The Autobiography of Alice B. Toklas*, "The old life was over" (142).

While visiting Alfred and Evelyn Whitehead in

Lockridge, England in the fall of 1914, Gertrude and Alice learned that war had broken out. Returning home in October, they found a dreary and depressed Paris and after a long cold winter, they decided to spend the spring and summer of 1915 in Majorca. On this Mediterranean island full of fig trees, views of the ocean, ships in the distance, a German war ship in the harbor, birds, fish, almonds, and sun, Gertrude began composing *Lifting Belly.*

Gertrude and Alice lived in Majorca until the winter of 1916 when they left for Paris to help with the war effort. One of Gertrude's American relatives sent them a Ford, which they named Aunt Pauline after Gertrude's Aunt "who behaved fairly well most times if she was properly flattered" (*The Autobiography of Alice B. Toklas,* 173). William Cook, an artist friend of Gertrude's, taught her to drive. Alice's comment on Gertrude's driving was that: "She goes forward admirably, she does not go backwards successfully" (*The Autobiography,* 173) — a perfect metaphor for Stein's life and writing. With their new car, Gertrude and Alice joined the American Fund for French Wounded (A.F.F.W.).

Gertrude drove. Alice did everything else. Their first job was to deliver hospital supplies to forces in Perpignan in the South of France. They drove long hours through the snow in a less than reliable vehicle. When they returned to Paris, they were sent to Nîmes, where they toured Roman ruins with a young American soldier who they nicknamed "Kiddie." During this time, when women were called upon to use their capacities to their fullest, when they felt needed and useful, when they experienced adventure and hardship, Gertrude continued writing

Lifting Belly. In 1917, with war raging around her, Gertrude completed *Lifting Belly*. In 1918 the world was still at war. In 1919 the war was over.

Gertrude drove. Alice did everything else. The relationship between Alice and Gertrude has been called hierarchical, heterosexual, and patriarchal and through our modern-day, feminist lens their love affair may appear this way. Yet, while we know that Alice took care of running the household — every detail, from ordering food to arranging visitors to keeping away distractions — there is another, much more important, aspect to Gertrude's relationship with Alice:

> She was not only Gertrude's typist and protector from all the disagreeable and distracting elements of life. She was also, most important, Gertrude's audience—and for a long time, Gertrude's only audience. . . . Gertrude's work, when it is successful, is a dance—but a dance that needs a partner. Where her work is exciting, which it often is, it is not because of the mere presence of the writing, but because of its teasing half-presence, and its invitation to join this dance. . . . The seductiveness of this invitation could not have been present in Gertrude's work had she written for herself alone, or even for 'herself and strangers'. She wrote most of the time, in those early days, for Alice, who read each day what Gertrude called the 'daily miracle,' and responded, typed each day. (Janet Hobhouse, *Everybody Who Was Anybody*, 93)

Late at night, after everyone had gone to bed, Gertrude wrote freely and full of excitement, filling school notebooks, some of them purple, some green, some black. Gertrude writes over and between the lines and when she is particularly excited, the words seem literally to dance, to fly off the page in big full sweeps, several words filling the whole page. Stein makes love to the paper, to the pencil — "Lifting belly pencils to me./ And pens." — to her audience, to Alice as she writes.

In the morning, while Gertrude slept, Alice picked up these pages and typed them. Later, when Gertrude arose, they compared the manuscript pages and the typed version. Alice questioned. Gertrude clarified and the work emerged. With Alice, to Alice, for Alice with Gertrude, by Alice to Gertrude, for Alice, Gertrude wrote *Lifting Belly*. It is the story of relationship, not one voice but voices — collaboration, dialogue, response, love.

> You write a book . . . you know you will be laughed at or pitied by everyone and you have a queer feeling and you are not very certain and you go on writing. Then some one says yes to it, to something you are liking, or doing or making and then never again can you have completely such a feeling of being afraid and ashamed that you had then when you were writing or liking the thing and not any one had said yes about the thing. (*The Making of Americans*, 485)

When *Lifting Belly* was first published in *Bee

Time Vine in 1953, reviewers ignored the work. Modern critics have generally been silent or condescending in their responses. Richard Bridgman, one of the few critics who even mentions *Lifting Belly*, Richard Bridgman writes:

> Physical passion had been virtually absent from Gertrude Stein's work since *The Making of Americans*, or at least, sufficiently disguised to be invisible. Now though, as she entered her forties, the demon of noon capered openly through her writing.
>
> The key erotic work of this period is "Lifting Belly" a fifty page love lyric composed mostly of one line tributes to "lifting belly." These are often followed by a cool and even sardonic response. Virgil Thomson has described it as concerning "The domestic 'affections,' " ("Lifting Belly," *BTV*, 64) and so it is, luridly so. (*Gertrude Stein in Pieces*, 149–150)

In the same passage he writes: "Gertrude Stein thought of her relationship with Alice B. Toklas in heterosexual terms" (149–150) and, "Even as she approached her fifties, Gertrude Stein's need to record her passions remained unquenchable" (150). Bridgman goes on to speculate that "at a time of considerable insecurity in Gertrude Stein's life" . . . "her aesthetic advances were overshadowed by autobiographical details" (150). Needless to say Bridgman's comments are disturbing, luridly so. To separate autobiographical details from aesthetic advances and to reduce Stein's expansive exploration of lesbian sexuality to the term "heterosexual" is to completely misunderstand the nature of *Lifting Belly*.

By associating lifting belly with the details of her everyday life — sandals, candles, figs, salmon, pencils — and with events, people and places all over the world — Geneva, Barcelona, the Battle of Verdun, The King and Queen of Montenegro — Stein creates a universe of lifting belly. Lifting belly is not lesbian sex, over there in the closet, hidden in bed, away from the public eye. Lifting belly is lesbian sex in the world, participating, relating and transforming everything it encounters. Lifting belly is a language. Lifting belly is an occupation. Lifting belly naturally celebrates. Lifting belly eroticizes, incarnates everything it touches. In the universe of lifting belly there is no separation between the personal and the aesthetic and the terms "heterosexual" and "homosexual" are meaningless.

Elizabeth Fifer in a more recent article, "Is Flesh Desirable" writes "Alice pleases in the subordinate position, 'as an apprentice' (8) to a great man Caesar or Seneca or a Gertrude Stein, who 'loved to be wed'." (*Signs: Journal of Women in Culture and Society* Spring, 1979, Vol. 4, Number 3, 472) There is no indication in the poem of a hierarchy between Stein and Toklas. In the poem Stein says that lifting belly is Baby, Alice's nickname for Gertrude and she says lifting belly is Pussy, Gertrude's nickname for Alice. Lifting belly is relationship. By repeating lifting belly over and over Stein puts her in every possible position, every possible relation; in *Lifting Belly* there is no subordinate position, only association. Caesar, a name people called Stein, becomes a complex sexual coding under the transforming power of lifting belly.

If we want to be true to Stein's work we must escape at least two impulses: one is searching for sexual equivalences and the other is ignoring the sexual nature of the work altogether. These impulses mirror the social reaction to lesbianism: lesbian either becomes synonymous with sex or does not exist. When reading *Lifting Belly* we can think we have found the meaning of a particular word — "Cows seem to be synonymous with orgasms" (Appendix to *The Biography of Alice B. Toklas,* "A Word about Caesars and Cows" 317) — when there are actually many meanings, as many as we can think of, as many as we have lived.

By performing the seemingly simple act of repeating the phrase "lifting belly" in all of the ways she can imagine; by freeing words so that they can be understood orally, not just visually — carnation becomes a flower and a nation of cars, sea becomes an ocean, "see," and the letter c; by inviting the objects of her every day life, the events on the news, birds and fish and trees and rain, history, myth, household objects, food, to inhabit her landscape, Gertrude Stein performs linguistic miracles. That which once reduced, oppressed, trivialized or obliterated female creativity/sexuality becomes female creativity. The reductive symbols used to define and confine women, "rose," "mother," "bride," "cow," "moon," find life again in relation to lifting belly. The patriarchal symbols of man — "sun," "general," "king," "Caesar," "war," "Ford," "monument" lose their power to dominate and find life again in relation to lifting belly. Dualities disappear in the relational world of lifting belly.

There are many ways to make love to lifting belly.

I will share one way — there are others, as many as we can live. As I read the first two pages of *Lifting Belly*, I hear Stein in labor struggling to lift belly, to bring her silenced sexuality into language. As I read "Part II," I hear Stein creating a language which will strengthen, nourish and encourage lifting belly. As I read "II," I hear Stein lifting belly without restraint, freeing her sexuality to occupy the universe, to cry out, to celebrate: "Kiss my lips. She did./ Kiss my lips again she did./ Kiss my lips over and over and over again she did" (20). I offer you my love letter to the first pages of lifting belly. In these pages, Gertrude sets the stage for the birth of lifting belly, hears the voices of those who want to keep lifting belly from being born, and finds a way to keep writing, to keep making love to Alice, while the patriarchal bombs of western culture literally and figuratively explode around her.

As I read the first words of the poem — "I have been heavy and had much selecting. I saw a star which was low. It was so low it twinkled. Breath was in it. Little pieces can be stupid" (1) — I breathe deeply. I respond to the meaning of the words: the sadness of being heavy and having to select. I also respond to the sound, rhythm, and feel of the words in my mouth, and the sight of the words on the paper. I experience the change in my breath as I read the short sentences and the two longer sentences, breathing at each period. I remember what it feels like to fall in love, to be short of breath, to breathe heavily when I am making love. I am breathing as I read. I am alive. Stein's writing is alive.

Stein is heavy with the weight lying on her, the dusty old books telling her that female sexuality is either precious and frail or evil and dangerous. She is also heavy with the weight of what is lying in her, the weight of this poem in her belly. She is heavy and full with love, with the desire to express her love. She is excited and she is pregnant. When Stein lets go of selecting, of censoring herself, she feels light and sees a star that is too low, and needs lifting. She is this star. Lesbian sexuality is this star. Woman's belly is this star. As she sees this star with breath and life in it, any little piece, any little idea, anything that is not this *whole* star seems stupid. She has had much — too much — selecting, too much silencing of her own voice, and now she sees a star which beckons her to the fire — "I want to tell about fire," — the fire of passion and anger, of life and destruction, a Phoenix burning the old and giving birth to the new: "We can understand heating and burning composition. Heating with wood" (1). With the wood of her pencil, with the fire in her belly, like an ancient alchemist Stein heats, and burns what has been composed, and she burns as she composes.

Fire is life. Breath is fire. "Fire is that which we have when we have olive" (1). The olive branch is the emblem of peace. Fire, love, passion is what we have when we have peace. In order to write *Lifting Belly* Stein must find peace, peace within herself and a place in the world where the war is not raging. She must create a place where she can make love and give birth: "Olive is a wood. We like linen. Linen is ordered. We are going to order linen" (1). When I read this line, I hear Alice and Gertrude ordering linen for their house in Majorca. I also hear Gertrude setting the stage for the birth of lifting belly. Linen for eating. Linen for the bed. Linen for lying in.

Linen for kissing. Lifting belly needs comfort, sleep, nourishment and quiet, as well as fire, to flourish. The stage is set.

Fire, wood, olive, linen, stars. "All belly belly well" (1). In this place, that is at once the scene of conception and death, all is well and all is the well of the belly, the ink well in which to dip one's pen. Pen, drink deeply in the well of the belly to write about our sexuality. Olive wood. O Live. Oh live. Alive. A live wood. A live word. Fire is what we have when we are alive. Oh live, Gertrude and lifting belly. Live. This is Stein's landscape, her territory. She is the creator. Alice is the creator. We are the creators. We can "*decide* upon wind," "*decide* that there will be stars and perhaps thunder and perhaps rain and perhaps no moon. Sometimes we decide that there will be a storm and rain. Sometimes we look at the boats. When we read about a boat we know that it has been sunk" (1–2).

Even as Gertrude claims her rights as a creator, she understands the destructive, patriarchal powers that lie out in the waters waiting to sink her vessel, to keep her from lifting belly. In Majorca in 1916, when Gertrude and Alice read about a boat in the newspaper, it was often a ship that had been sunk by German submarines. But the boat Stein mentions in the poem is a metaphorical boat, a boat of creation. These boats are ideas, that sail out onto the open seas. The "boats" that they read about, that the critics comment on, are sunk by their words. Stein knows that male words have sunk the belly of woman many times. Aware of this danger, she speaks to herself, to Alice, to all lesbians, to all women, to the poem itself: "Be alright. Be careful" (2). And then the line which guides me even as I write this introduction: "Say what you think" (2). I doing this, she gives lifting belly a voice. Lifting belly becomes an identity.

She goes on to tell *Lifting Belly*, "Belief in there being the same kind of dog." In *The Geographical History of America,* Stein writes "I am I because my little dog knows me" (110). Stein must have "Belief in there being the same kind of dog," the person who is like her, in order to keep writing. But this line also warns us that there may be a "dog" an identity, an interloper who wants to intrude and that we must, "Jerk him away" (2), "Answer that you do not care to think so" (2). She says that she has shown "you," meaning both her readers and herself "the road" or how to write about our sexuality and survive. She has given us a map.

At this moment in the writing Stein experiences the jerk, the diversion, the memory of her quarrel with a man, perhaps Leo, and she must follow her own advice. Stein is "alright," "careful," "angry" and she "says what she thinks." She is "alright," not in any danger, because she "showed him the road," meaning she told him to leave. She is careful because she will not let him take over her narrative. She will forget. She is angry because she showed him the road, meaning this time that she showed him her ideas, her writing, the meaning of Cubism or Modernism and he did not thank her. She is angry and would like him to thank her: "Ask him to thank me" (2). Finally, she says what she thinks: "I don't pardon him. I find him objectionable" (2). Stein and *Lifting Belly* are alright.

This interruption does, however, upset lifting belly

and she disappears. Too much attention to anger at men will make lesbian sexuality disappear: "What is it when it's upset. It isn't in the room" (2). Stein must bring in the moonlight, the darkness, sleep, night, all traditionally feminine symbols, to bring lifting belly back into the room. The lover, the language of the poem, requires continual attention. As *Lifting Belly* is coming into form, Stein finds the support of other voices, of many voices. These voices tell her "Say it" (2). "You didn't say it" (2). Be clear. Don't be misunderstood. She creates an other, Alice, an audience, who is not only listening, but demands precision. If she were speaking into the void she could not write.

And her other, the one and the other asks: "Do you lift everybody in that way./ No" (2). This poem is not for everybody. Again she shows us the road, as lifting belly shows her the road. "You are to say No" (2). At this moment lifting belly is strong enough to meet her audience.

> How are you.
> Lifting belly how are you lifting belly.
> We like a fire and we don't mind if it smokes.
> Do you.
> How do you do. The Englishmen are coming. Not here. No an Englishwoman. An Englishman and an Englishwoman (2–3).

Stein tells lifting belly what Alice and her, what the lovers, what lesbians, want from lifting belly. We like a fire and we don't mind if it smokes. We like fire — passion — and we don't mind if people can see the smoke. We don't mind if people know about our sexuality. We will let them see the fire of our lives. We are also just like everyone else. We like to sit in our house and have a fire when we are making love: "Do you." Do you? They want to know do we, does lifting belly, do all the women who understand, do all the other lesbians, do they like a fire? Then she asks politely "How do you do." which means simultaneously: how is lifting belly done? how do you make love with your lover? how do you lift the belly, the creativity of women? how do you write about lifting belly and simply how do you do? — nice to meet you.

At the very moment when lifting belly is making her debut, the Englishmen arrive: "The Englishmen are coming." The words "Not here" are the protest, the anger. If the Englishmen appear in this coded, lesbian world, lifting belly might sink. If friends visit while Alice and Gertrude are making love they interrupt the passion. But in this fertile, mythic place of moonlight and darkness, wind and thunder, rain and stars, the Englishmen and the Englishwomen, the censors of female passion, will come forward to challenge the strength of lifting belly and Stein will show them the road. It is not an Englishman. It is an Englishwoman, but no, it is both. It is the men and women of English. They have come to correct Gertrude's grammar: "What did you say lifting belly? I did not understand you correctly. It is not well said. For lifting belly. For lifting belly not to lifting belly" (3).

Yet even at this moment when Stein hears the

voices of her censors — "it is not well said" — she also strains to hear the voice of lifting belly: "What did you say lifting belly?" She is writing *for* lifting belly, not *to* lifting belly. Lifting belly asks for its other name and Stein says it is representative. Of what? She answers "the evils of eating" (3). She embodies and thus saves lifting belly by using the metaphor for oral sex, "eating," a word connecting us back to our tongues and our bellies, back to eating, making love, giving birth, speaking, back to fire and breath.

This other "sin," the indulgence in sweets and figs, averts the disaster and we move from "not well said" to Yes: "Yes we will it will be very easy" (3). It will be easy to talk about this other lifting belly. To talk about lifting belly in this other way. From this point on lifting belly keeps meeting and eating and digesting all the words that the Englishmen and women, that Western culture, uses to define sexuality. Gradually all that once seemed dangerous, that once threatened to sink lifting belly, becomes lifting belly. Lifting Belly. Be alright. Yes.

Stein often repeats the words: "Lifting belly is so strong." She also repeats the words, "Lifting belly is so kind." Lifting belly must be both kind and strong, fire and linen, fierce and tender.

Part II
Lifting belly. Are you. Lifting.

Oh dear I said. I was tender, fierce and tender.

Do it. What a splendid example of carelessness.

It gives me a great deal of pleasure to say
yes.
Why do I always smile.
I don't know. (3)

Lifting belly has made it through the rough
waters. Stein has said "Yes to lifting belly. Lifting
belly has said Yes to Stein. Lifting belly is born and
lifting belly is always being born. Each time Stein
introduces one of the powerful symbols from Western
culture into the universe of lifting belly, lifting belly
expands to include and thus transform this symbol.

"Lifting belly and roses/ We get a great many
roses" (4). Roses are not only the traditional symbol
of female sexuality in lyric love poetry, they are the
romantic token which a man sends a woman to
express his love. How can lifting belly deal with
roses? Stein approaches this powerful symbol by first
writing about other flowers, about lilies, petunias and
pansies and then she says what she thinks: "I don't
see how you can write on the wall about roses" (8).
In the Book of Daniel 5:24, when the King reads the
writing on the wall, he knows that his reign is over.
At first, Stein does not see how to end the reign of
the rose, a dangerous situation for lifting belly. The
line "Lifting belly, a terminus" (8), an end, shows
that if the rose continues to define female sexuality,
if the line "A rose is a rose is a rose" continues to
define and confine Gertrude Stein, then Stein will not
be able to keep writing lifting belly.

But the word "terminus" does not have to mean
end. Terminus. Term in us. Lifting belly is a term, a
word, that is within us, within our bellies. Lifting
belly is a term, a term of pregnancy. Gertrude and

Alice had "a rose is a rose is a rose is a rose" written circularly on the ceiling above their bed, on the "wall." This was Alice's idea. Gertrude is talking to Alice. She is wondering how she can live with this now solid phrase. She makes rose a term in us, in her, a word living in her. She takes the object, the writing on the wall and makes the rose live again. Lifting belly breathes life into everything it touches.

Stein can return to her famous line, from "Sacred Emily" and give it new meaning: "Lifting belly can please me because it is an occupation I enjoy. /Rose is a rose is a rose is a rose" (39). A rose is a rose is a rose in all its meanings, not only as a symbol for women' sexuality in male poetry, not only as the flowers sent to Gertrude and Alice. A red rose, a wet rose, a pussy rose. A rose is the past participle of arise which means to get up [to wake up, to wake up from "Sleep and not sleep. We sleep every night" (2)] — to be aroused sexually.

> I do love roses and carnations.
> A mistake. There can be no mistakes.
> I do not say a mother.
> Lifting belly
> Lifting belly.
> Cry.
> Lifting belly.
> Lifting belly
> Splendid. (17–18)

At the mention of the word "mother," lifting belly cries. Cry lifting belly. Cry. Cry. Cry for what is not. Cry for women's sexuality which has been reduced to motherhood. Cry for the baby that does not come from lesbian lovemaking. Cry. But then, cry lifting belly. Cry out lifting belly. Splendid. Cry out for the mother that you are. Cry out as you give birth. Cry out for the lover that you are. Cry out as you feel your fire.

A star led Stein to find lifting belly. While a star led the three wise men to the birth of Christ, Mary did not lift her belly to give birth. She was only a vessel. The baby was a miracle. In *Lifting Belly* Stein actively lifts her belly. The baby is a miracle.

> Because lifting belly is about baby.
> Three eggs in lifting belly.
> Eclair.
> Think of it.
> Think of that.
> We think of that. (55)

As I have mentioned before, Alice's nickname for Gertrude was "baby," Gertrude's nickname for Alice was "Pussy." *Lifting Belly* is about Gertrude, about Baby, but *Lifting Belly,* the poem, is also a baby: the creation of life arising from the union of Alice and Gertrude. "There are three eggs in lifting belly." There are three l's in the words "lifting belly." There are three "elles," the French pronoun for she, in lifting belly. There are three women and there are three eggs in these three women. There are two women and a baby. Baby is Alice's nickname for Gertrude. Baby is creation. There is each woman and there are the two together, there is lesbian lovemaking — how do you do — the baby. Lifting belly is the lovemaking.

Eclair. Is this clear? Eclair. The pastry, the sweet, is made with two pieces of pastry with cream in the middle. Two women together aroused. One woman aroused. Think of it. Think of that. It is lifting belly. That is lifting belly. We think of that. We think of lifting belly and we think of food, of figs, and strawberries, and eclairs and Caesar salads.

Alice made delicious Caesar salads. Gertrude ate them. Alice and Gertrude toured the Roman ruins around Nîmes while Gertrude was writing *Lifting Belly*. Caesar was a Roman general. Many people called Stein Caesar because they thought she looked like a Roman General:

> I say lifting belly and then I say lifting belly and Caesars. I say lifting belly gently and Caesars gently. I say lifting belly again and Caesars again. I say lifting belly and I say Caesars and I say lifting belly Caesars and cow come out. I say lifting belly and Caesars and cow come out.
>
> Can you read my print.
>
> Lifting belly say can you see the Caesars. I can see what I kiss.
>
> Of course you can.
>
> Lifting belly high.
>
> That is what I adore always more and more.
>
> Come out cow.
>
> Little connections.
>
> Yes oh yes cow come out.
>
> Lifting belly unerringly.
>
> A wonderful book

Baby my baby I backhand for thee.
She is a sweet baby and well baby and me.
(33)

When you listen to this passage, think of Caesar
not only as a general, as Gertrude, as a salad, but as
cease her, seize her, sees her, and finally as seizure, a
tremor during sex, an orgasm. If Caesar is all of
these, then it is all at once, burning and heating, the
death and the renewal, the ceasing and the seizure,
the pleasure. If Caesar is an orgasm, the lover can
see the Caesar as she is going down on her. She is
kissing it. "I can see what I kiss." At the same time,
she can read her print, she can understand Caesar,
her real identity, because she can kiss her, because
she loves her, because she sees her and does not want
to cease or seize her. And we can understand that we
are kissing her, because we have kissed each other.
She can endure and triumph in the face of war and
generals. She is a sweet baby and a well baby.

In *Lifting Belly* Stein says these three sentences
in the following order: "When this you see remember
me" (26). "When this you see believe me" (31).
"When this you see you will kiss me" (54). Stein
moves from embracing writing as a source of personal
fulfillment — immortality — to writing as a gift to
future lesbians who will see ourselves in the writing
and will kiss Stein for the empowering celebration of
our sexuality which she has given us. Stein can write
and we can agree: "What did I say, that I was a
great poet like the English only sweeter" (23). Stein
is a great poet and she has given lesbians a great
gift. She has given us the vision of an uncloseted,

joyous sexuality, powerful enough to celebrate splendidly, to survive even in a world at war.

Having overcome the obstacles to writing the most passionate, most deeply felt truths about her body, about the belly of creation, Stein offers us her breath and her fire. I have shared the story I hear when I read *Lifting Belly*. There are many ways to make love to *Lifting Belly*. Read her aloud. Take her to bed with a friend. Take her to bed alone. Take her to the sea. Read her aloud with a whole group of friends. Read her in pieces. Read her in one setting. Read her for the sound of the words. Read her for the story line. Read her for the humor. Read her for the sensuous imagery. Read her and listen to words echoing with one another. Read her as music. Lifting belly is a baby and a wonderful book. "Little connections." Lifting belly. "Lifting belly I love cherish idolize, adore and worship you. You are so sweet, so tender, and so perfect" (19).

> In the meantime listen to Miss Cheatham
> In the midst of writing
> In the midst of writing there is merriment.
(62)

Works Cited

Bridgman, Richard, *Gertrude Stein in Pieces*. *New York: Oxford University Press, 1971*.

Hobhouse, Janet, *Everybody Who Was Anybody: A Biography of Gertrude Stein*. New York: Putnam's Sons, 1975.

Simon, Linda. *The Biography of Alice B. Toklas*. Garden City: Doubleday, 1977.

Stein, Gertrude. *The Autobiography of Alice B. Toklas*. New York: Vintage Books, 1961.

————. *Bee Time Vine and Other Pieces [1913–1927]*. New York: Books for Libraries Press, 1953.

————. *Fernhurst, Q.E.D. and Other Early Writings*. New York: Liveright, 1971.

————. *The Geographical History of America; or The Relation of Human Nature to the Human Mind*. New York: Vintage Books, 1973.

————. *The Making of Americans: Being the History of a Family's Progress*. London: Peter Owen, 1968.

————. *The Yale Gertrude Stein*. Selections with and Introduction by Richard Kostelanetz. New Haven: Yale University Press, 1980.

————. *Three Lives*. New York: Vintage, 1936.

I have been heavy and had much selecting. I saw a star which was low. It was so low it twinkled. Breath was in it. Little pieces are stupid.

I want to tell about fire. Fire is that which we have when we have olive. Olive is a wood. We like linen. Linen is ordered. We are going to order linen.

· All belly belly well.

Bed of coals made out of wood.

I think this one may be an expression. We can understand heating and burning composition. Heating with wood.

Sometimes we readily decide upon wind we decide that there will be stars and perhaps thunder and perhaps rain and perhaps no moon. Sometimes we decide that there will be a storm and rain. Sometimes we look at the boats. When we read about a boat we know that it has been sunk. Not by the waves but by the sails. Any one knows that rowing is dangerous. Be alright. Be careful. Be angry. Say what you think. Believe in there being the same kind of a dog. Jerk. Jerk him away. Answer that you do not care to think so.

We quarreled with him. We quarreled with him then. Do not forget that I showed you the road. Do not forget that I showed you the road. We will forget it because he does not oblige himself to thank me. Ask him to thank me.

The next time that he came we offered him something to read. There is a great difference of opinion as to whether cooking in oil is or is not healthful.

I don't pardon him. I find him objectionable.

What is it when it's upset. It isn't in the room. Moonlight and darkness. Sleep and not sleep. We sleep every night.

What was it.

I said lifting belly.

You didn't say it.

I said it I mean lifting belly.

Don't misunderstand me.

Do you.

Do you lift everybody in that way.

No.

You are to say No.

Lifting belly.

How are you.

Lifting belly how are you lifting belly.

We like a fire and we don't mind if it smokes.

Do you.

How do you do. The Englishmen are coming. Not here. No an Englishwoman. An Englishman and an Englishwoman.

What did you say lifting belly. I did not understand you correctly. It is not well said. For lifting belly. For lifting belly not to lifting belly.

Did you say, oh lifting belly.

What is my another name.

Representative.

Of what.

Of the evils of eating.

What are they then.

They are sweet and figs.

Do not send them.

Yes we will it will be very easy.

PART II

Lifting belly. Are you. Lifting.

Oh dear I said I was tender, fierce and tender.

Do it. What a splendid example of carelessness.

It gives me a great deal of pleasure to say yes.

Why do I always smile.

I don't know.

It pleases me.

You are easily pleased.

I am very pleased.

Thank you I am scarcely sunny.

I wish the sun would come out.

Yes.

Do you lift it.

High.

Yes sir I helped to do it.

Did you.

Yes.
Do you lift it.
We cut strangely.
What.
That's it.
Address it say to it that we will never repent.
A great many people come together.
Come together.
I don't think this has anything to do with it.
What I believe in is what I mean.
Lifting belly and roses.
We get a great many roses.
I always smile.
Yes.
And I am happy.
With what.
With what I said.
This evening.
Not pretty.
Beautiful.
Yes beautiful.
Why don't you prettily bow.
Because it shows thought.
It does.
Lifting belly is so strong.
A great many things are weaknesses. You are
pleased to so. I say because I am so well pleased.
With what. With what I said.
There are a great many weaknesses.
Lifting belly.
What was it I said.
I can add that.
It's not an excuse.

4

I do not like bites.
How lift it.
Not so high.
What a question.
I do not understand about ducks.
Do not you.
I don't mean to close.
No of course not.
Dear me. Lifting belly.
Dear me. Lifting belly.
Oh yes.
Alright.
Sing.
Do you hear.
Yes I hear.
Lifting belly is amiss.
This is not the way.
I see.
Lifting belly is alright.
Is it a name.
Yes it's a name.
We were right.
So you weren't pleased.
I see that we are pleased.
It is a great way.
To go.
No not to go.
But to lift.
Not light.
Paint.
No not paint.
All the time we are very happy.
All loud voices are seen. By whom. By the best.

Lifting belly is so erroneous.
I don't like to be teased and worried.
Lifting belly is so accurate.
Yes indeed.
She was educated.
And pleased.
Yes indeed.
Lifting belly is so strong.
I said that to mean that I was very glad.
Why are you very glad.
Because that pleased me.
Baby love.
A great many people are in the war.
I will go there and back again.
What did you say about Lifting belly.
I said lifting belly is so strong.
Yes indeed it is and agreeable and grateful.
We have gratitude.
No one can say we haven't.
Lifting belly is so cold. Not in summer. No nor in
winter either.
All of it is a joke.
Lifting belly is no joke. Not after all.
I am so discouraged about it. About lifting belly. I
question.
I am so discouraged about lifting belly.
The other day there was a good deal of sunlight.
There often is.
There often is here.
We are very well satisfied at present.
So enthusiastic.
Lifting belly has charm.
Charming.

Alright.
Lifting belly is not very interesting.
To you.
To me.
Say did you see that the wind was from the east.
It usually is from the South.
We like rain.
Sneeze. This is the way to say it.
You meant a pressure.
Indeed yes.
All the time there is a chance to see me. I don't
wish it to be said so.
The skirt.
And water.
You mean ocean water.
Not exactly an ocean a sea.
A success.
Was it a success.
Lifting belly is all there.
Lifting belly high.
It is not necessary to repeat the word.
How do you do I forgive you everything and there
is nothing to forgive.
Lifting belly is so high.
Do you like lilies.
Do you like lilies.
Use the word lifting belly is so high.
In place of that.
A special case to-day.
Of peaches.
Lifting belly is delightful.
Lifting belly is so high.
To-day.

Yes to-day.
Do you think that said yesterday.
Yes to-day.
Don't be silly.
In that we see that we can please me.
I don't see how you can write on the wall about roses.
Lifting belly a terminus.
What is there to please me.
Alright.
A pocket.
Lifting belly is good.
Rest.
Arrest.
Do you please m.
I do more than that.
When are you most proud of me.
Dare I ask you to be satisfied.
Dear me.
Lifting belly is anxious.
Not about Verdun.
Oh dear no.
The wind whistles that means it whistles just like any one. I thought it was a whistle.
Lifting belly together.
Do you like that there.
There are not mistakes made.
Not here at any rate.
Not here at any rate.
There are no mistakes made. Not here at any rate.
When do I see the lightning. Every night.
Lifting belly again.

It is a credit to me.

There was an instant of lifting belly.

Lifting belly is an occasion. An occasion to please me. Oh yes. Mention it.

Lifting belly is courteous.

Lifting belly is hilarious, gay and favorable.

Oh yes it is.

Indeed it is not a disappointment.

Not to me.

Lifting belly is such an incident. In one's life.

Lifting belly is such an incident in one's life.

I don't mean to be reasonable.

Shall I say thin.

This makes me smile.

Lifting belly is so kind.

A great many clouds for the sun. You mean the sun on high.

Leave me.

See me.

Lifting belly is no joke.

I appreciate that.

Do not show kindness.

Why not.

Because it ruffles me.

Do not say that it is unexpected.

Lifting belly is so scarce.

Not to-day.

Lifting belly is so kind.

To me there are many exceptional cases.

What did you say. I said I had not been disturbed. Neither had we. Lifting belly is so necessary.

Lifting belly is so kind.

I can't say it too often.

Pleasing me.
Lifting belly.
Extraordinary.
Lifting belly is such exercise.
You mean altogether.
Lifting belly is so kind to me.
Lifting belly is so kind to many.
Don't say that please.
If you please.
Lifting belly is right.
And we were right.
Now I say again. I say now again.
What is a whistle.
Miracle you don't know about the miracle.
You mean a meteor.
No I don't I mean everything away.
Away where.
Away here.
Oh yes.
Lifting belly is so strong.
You said that before.
Lifting belly is so strong and willing.
Lifting belly is so strong and yet waiting.
Lifting belly is so soothing. Yes indeed.
It gives me greater pleasure.
Does it.
It gives me great pleasure.
What do you mean by St. John.
A great many churches are visited.
Lifting belly try again.
I will not say what I think about lifting belly. Oh yes you will.

Well then please have it understood that I can't
be responsible for doubts. Nobody doubts.
Nobody doubts.
I have no use for lifting belly.
Do you say that to me.
No I don't.
Anybody who is wisely urged to go to Inca goes to
the hill.
What hill. The hill above lifting belly.
It is all hill.
Not very well.
Not very well hill.
Lifting belly is so strong.
And clear.
Why do you say feeding.
Lifting belly is such a windmill.
Do you stare.
Lifting belly to me.
What did he say.
He didn't say that he was waiting.
I have been adequately entertained.
Some when they sigh by accident say poor country
she is betrayed.
I didn't say that to-day. No indeed you didn't.
Mixing belly is so kind.
Lifting belly is so a measure of it all.
Lifting belly is a picnic.
On a fine day.
We like the weather it is very beautiful.
Lifting belly is so able.
Lifting belly is so able to be praised.
The act.

The action.
A great many people are excitable.
Mixing belly is so strange.
Lifting belly is so satisfying.
Do not speak to me.
Of it.
Lifting belly is so sweet.
That is the way to separate yourself from the
water.
Lifting belly is so kind.
Loud voices discuss pigeons.
Do loud voices discuss pigeons.
Remember me to the hill. What hill. The hill in
back of Genova.
Lifting belly is so kind. So very kind.
Lifting belly is so kind.
I never mean to insist to-day.
Lifting belly is so consecutive.
With all of us.
Lifting belly is so clear.
Very clear.
And there is lots of water.
Lifting belly is so impatient
So impatient to-day.
Lifting belly is all there.
Do I doubt it.
Lifting belly.
What are my plans.
There are some she don't mention.
There are some she doesn't mention. Some others
she doesn't mention.

Lifting belly is so careful. Full of care for me. Lifting belly is mean. I see. You mean lifting belly is all right.

Lifting belly is so simple.

Listen to me to-day.

Lifting belly is so warm.

Leave it to me.

Leave what to me.

Lifting belly is such an experiment.

We were thoroughly brilliant.

If I were a postman I would deliver letters. We call them letter carriers.

Lifting belly is so strong. And so judicious.

Lifting belly is an exercise.

Exercise is very good for me.

Lifting belly necessarily pleases the latter.

Lifting belly is necessary.

Do believe me.

Lifting belly quietly.

It is very exciting.

Stand.

Why do you stand.

Did you say you thought it would make any difference.

Lifting belly is not so kind.

Little places to sting.

We used to play star spangled banner.

Lifting belly is so near.

Lifting belly is so dear.

Lifting belly all around.

Lifting belly makes a sound.

Keep still.

Lifting belly is gratifying.

I can't express the hauntingness of Dugny.

I can't express either the obligation I have to say say it.

Lifting belly is so kind.

Dear me lifting belly is so kind.

Am I in it.

That doesn't affect it.

How do you mean.

Lifting belly and a resemblance.

There is no resemblance.

A plain case of misdeed.

Lifting belly is peaceable.

The Cataluna has come home.

Lifting belly is a success.

So is tenderness.

Lifting belly is kind and good and beautiful.

Lifting belly is my joy.

Do you believe in singling. Singing do you mean.

Lifting belly is a special pleasure.

Who can be convinced of this measure.

Lifting belly is perfect.

I know what you mean.

Lifting belly was very fatiguing.

Did you make a note of it of the two donkeys and the three dogs. The smaller one is the mother of the other two.

Lifting belly

Exactly.

Lifting belly all the time.

Do be careful of me.

Remarkably so.

Remarkably a recreation.
Lifting belly is so satisfying.
Lifting belly to me.
Large quantities of it.
Say that you see that you are praised.
Lifting belly.
See that.
You have entertained me.
Hurry up.
Hurry up with it.
Lifting belly does that astonish you.
Excuse me.
Why do you wish to hear me.
I wish to hear you because it pleases me.
Yesterday and to-day.
Yesterday and to-day we managed it altogether.
Lifting belly is so long.
It is an expression of opinion.
Conquistador. James I.
It is exceptional.
Lifting belly is current rolling. Lifting belly is so strong.
Lifting belly is so strong.
That is what I say.
I say it to please me.
Please yourself with thunder.
Lifting belly is famous.
So are many celebrations.
Lifting belly is so.
We mean lifting belly.
We mean it and do we care.
We keep all the letters.
Lifting belly is so seen.

15

You mean here.
Not with spy glasses.
Lifting belly is an expression.
Explain it explain it to me.
Lifting belly is cautious.
Of course these words are said.
To be strong.
Lifting belly.
Yes orchids.
Lifting belly is so adaptable.
That will amuse my baby.
Lifting belly is a way of sitting.
I don't mean to laugh.
Lifting belly is such a reason.
Lifting belly is such a reason.
Why do I say bench.
Because it is laughable.
Lifting belly is so droll.
We have met to-day with every kind of consideration.
Not very good. Of course it is very good.
Lifting belly is so kind.
Why do you say that.
Bouncing belly.
Did you say bouncing belly.
We asked here for a sister.
Lifting belly is not noisy.
We go to Barcelona to-morrow.
Lifting belly is an acquisition.
I forgot to put in a special cake. Love to be.
Very well.
Lifting belly is the understanding.
Sleepy.

Why do you wake up.
Lifting belly keep it.
We will send it off.
She should.
Nothing pleases me except dinner.
I have done as I wished and I do not feel any responsibility to you.
Are you there.
Lifting belly.
What do I say.
Pussy how pretty you are.
That goes very quickly unless you have been there too long.
I told him I would send him Mildred's book. He seemed very pleased at the prospect.
Lifting belly is so strong.
Lifting belly together.
Lifting belly oh yes.
Lifting belly.
Oh yes.
Remember what I say.
I have no occasion to deliberate.
He has not heart but that you can supply.
The fan goes alright
Lifting belly what is earnest. Expecting an arena to be monumental.
Lifting belly is recognised to be the only spectacle present. Do you mean that.
Lifting belly is a language. It says island. Island a strata. Lifting belly is a repetition.
Lifting belly means me.
I do love roses and carnations.
A mistake. There can be no mistakes.

I do not say a mother.
Lifting belly.
Lifting belly.
Cry.
Lifting belly.
Lifting belly. Splendid.
Jack Johnson Henry.
Henry is his name sir.
Jack Johnson Henry is an especially eloquent curtain.
We see a splendid force in mirrors.
Angry we are not angry.
Pleasing.
Lifting belly raining.
I am good looking.
A magazine of lifting belly. Excitement sisters.
Did we see the bird jelly I call it. I call it something religious. You mean beautiful. I do not know that I like large rocks. Sarsen land we call it. Oh yes. Lifting belly is a persuasion. You are satisfied. With it. With it and with you. I am satisfied with your behavior. I call it astonishing. Lifting belly is so exact and audible and Spanish curses. You know I prefer a bird. What bird. Why a yellow bird. I saw it first. That was an accident. You mean by accident. I mean exactly what I said. Lifting belly is a great luxury. Can you imitate a cow.
Lifting belly is so kind.
And so cold.
Lifting belly is a rare instance. I am fond of it. I am attached to the accentuation.
Lifting belly is a third.

Did you say third. No I said Avila.

Listen to him sing.

She is so sweet and thrilling.

Listen to me as yet I have no color. Red white and blue all out but you.

This is the best thing I have ever said. Lifting belly and it, it is not startling. Lifting belly until to-morrow. Lifting belly to-morrow.

I would not be surprised surprised if I added that yet.

Lifting belly to me.

I am fondest of all of lifting belly.

Lifting belly careful don't say anything about lifting belly.

I did not change my mind.

Neither did you carefully.

Lifting belly and again lifting belly.

I have changed my mind about the country.

Lifting belly and action and voices and care to be taken.

Does it make any difference if you pay for paper or not.

Listen to me. Using old automobile tires as sandals is singularly interesting. It is done in Avila.

What did I tell. Lifting belly is so kind.

What kind of a noise does it make. Like the man at night. The man that calls out. We hear him.

Lifting belly is so strong. I love cherish idolise adore and worship you. You are so sweet so tender and so perfect.

Did you believe in sandals. When they are made of old automobile tire. I wish I knew the history of it.

Lifting belly is notorious.

A great many people wish to salute. The general does. So does the leader of the battalion. In spanish. I understand that.

I understand everything.

Lifting belly is to jelly.

Holy most is in the sky.

We see it in three.

Yes we see it every night near the hills. This is so natural. Birds do it. We do not know their name.

Lifting belly or all I can never be pleased with this. Listen to me. Lifting belly is so kind.

Lifting belly is so dear.

Lifting belly is here.

Did we not hear and we were walking leave it to me and say some quickly now. He is not sleepy. At last I know why he laughs. Do you.

I will not imitate colors. From the stand point of white yellow is colored. Do you mean bushes. No I mean acacias. Lilacs do fade. What did you say for lifting belly. Extra. Extra thunder. I can so easily be fastidious.

II

Kiss my lips. She did.

Kiss my lips again she did.

Kiss my lips over and over and over again she did.

I have feathers.

Gentle fishes.

Do you think about apricots. We find them very beautiful. It is not alone their color it is their seeds that charm us. We find it a change.

Lifting belly is so strange.
I came to speak about it.
Selected raisins well their grapes grapes are good.
Change your name.
Question and garden.
It's raining. Don't speak about it.
My baby is a dumpling. I want to tell her something.
Wax candles. We have bought a great many wax candles. Some are decorated. They have not been lighted.
I do not mention roses.
Exactly.
Actually.
Question and butter.
I find the butter very good.
Lifting belly is so kind.
Lifting belly fattily.
Doesn't that astonish you.
You did want me.
Say it again.
Strawberry.
Lifting beside belly.
Lifting kindly belly.
Sing to me I say.
Some are wives not heroes.
Lifting belly merely.
Sing to me I say.
Lifting belly. A reflection.
Lifting belly adjoins more prizes.
Fit to be.
I have fit on a hat.
Have you.

What did you say to excuse me. Difficult paper and scattered.

Lifting belly is so kind.

What shall you say about that. Lifting belly is so kind.

What is a veteran.

A veteran is one who has fought.

Who is the best.

The king and the queen and the mistress.

Nobody has a mistress.

Lifting belly is so kind.

To-day we decided to forgive Nellie.

Anybody can describe dresses.

How do you do what is the news.

Lifting belly is so kind.

Lifting belly exactly.

The king and the prince of Montenegro.

Lifting belly is so kind.

Lifting belly to please me.

Excited.

Excited are you.

I can whistle, the train can whistle whistle we can hear the whistle, the boat whistle. The train is not running to-day. Mary whistle whistle for the whim.

Didn't you say you'd write it better.

Mrs. Vettie. It is necessary to have a Ford.

Yes sir.

Dear Mrs. Vettie. Smile to me.

I am.

Dear Mrs. Vettie never better.

Yes indeed so.

Lifting belly is most kind.

What did I say, that I was a great poet like the English only sweeter.

When I think of this afternoon and the garden I see what you mean.

You are not thinking of the pleasure.

Lifting belly again.

What did I mention when I drew a pansy that pansy and petunia both begin with p.

Lifting belly splendidly.

We have wishes.

Let us say we know it.

Did I say anything about it. I know the tittle. We know the title.

Lifting belly is so kind.

We have made no mistake.

The Montenegrin family.

A condition to a wide admiration.

Lifting belly after all.

You don't mean disobedience.

Lifting belly all around.

Eat the little girl I say.

Listen to me. Did you expect it to go back. Why do you do to stop.

What do you do to stop.

What do you do to go on.

I do the same.

Yes wishes. Oh yes wishes.

What do you do to turn a corner.

What do you do to sing.

We don't mention singing.

What do you do to be reformed.

You know.

Yes wishes.
What do you do to measure.
I do it in such a way.
I hope to see them come.
Lifting belly go around.
I was sorry to be blistered.
We were such company.
Did she say jelly.
Jelly my jelly.
Lifting belly is so round.
Big Caesars.
Two Caesars.
Little seize her.
Too.
Did I do my duty.
Did I wet my knife.
No I don't mean whet.
Exactly four teeth.
Little belly is so kind.
What did you say about accepting.
Yes.
Lifting belly another lifting belly.
I question the weather.
It is not necessary.
Lifting belly oh lifting belly in time.
Yes indeed.
Be to me.
Did you say this was this.
Mr. Louis.
Do not mention Mr. Louis.
Little axes.
Yes indeed little axes and rubbers.
This is a description of an automobile.

I understand all about them.
Lifting belly is so kind.
So is whistling.
A great many whistles are shrill.
Lifting belly connects.
Lifting belly again.
Sympathetic blessing.
Not curls.
Plenty of wishes.
All of them fulfilled.
Lifting belly you don't say so.
Climb trees.
Lifting belly has sparks.
Sparks of anger and money.
Lifting belly naturally celebrates
We naturally celebrate.
Connect me in places.
Lifting belly.
No no don't say that.
Lifting belly oh yes.
Tax this.
Running behind a mountain.
I fly to thee.
Lifting belly.
Shall I chat.
I mean pugilists.
Oh yes trainer.
Oh yes yes.
Say it again to study.
It has been perfectly fed.
Oh yes I do.
Belly alright.
Lifting belly very well.

Lifting belly this.

So sweet.

To me.

Say anything a mudding made of Caesars.

Lobster. Baby is so good to baby.

I correct blushes. You mean wishes.

I collect pearls. Yes and colors.

All colors are gods. Oh yes Beddlington.

Now I collect songs.

Lifting belly is so nice.

I wrote about it to him.

I wrote about it to her.

Not likely not very likely that they will seize rubber. Not very likely that they will seize rubber.

Lifting belly yesterday.

And to-day.

And to-morrow.

A train to-morrow.

Lifting belly is so exciting.

Lifting belly asks any more.

Lifting belly captures.

Seating.

Have a swim.

Lifting belly excuses.

Can you swim.

Lifting belly for me.

When this you see remember me.

Oh yes.

Yes.

Researches and a cab.

A cab right.

Lifting belly phlegmatically.

Bathing bathing in bliss.

I am very well satisfied with meat.
Kindness to my wife.
Lifting belly to a throne.
Search it for me.
Yes wishes.
I say it again I am perfection in behavior and circumstance.
Oh yes alright.
Levelheaded fattuski.
I do not wish to be Polish.
Quite right in singing.
Lifting belly is so recherché.
Lifting belly.
Up.
Correct me.
I believe he makes together of pieces.
Lifting belly.
Not that.
Think of me.
Oh yes.
Lifting belly for me.
Right there.
Not that yesterday.
Fetch missions.
Lifting belly or Dora.
Lifting belly.
Yes Misses.
Lifting belly separately all day.
I say lifting belly.
An example.
A good example.
Cut me a slice.
You see what I wish.

I wish a seat and Caesar.
Caesar is plural.
I can think.
And so can I.
And argue.
Oh yes you see.
What I see.
You see me.
Yes stretches.
Stretches and stretches of happiness.
Should you have put it away.
Yes you should have put it away.
Do not think so much.
I do not.
Have you a new title.
Lifting belly articulately.
It is not a problem.
Kissing and singing.
We have the habit when we wash.
In singing we say how do you do how do you like
the war.
Little dumps of it.
Did you hear that man. What did he say close it.
Lifting belly lifting pleasure.
What can we say about wings.
Wings and refinement.
Come to me.
Sleepy.
Sleepily we think.
Wings after lunch.
I don't think.
No don't I regret a silver sugar.
And I platinum knitting needles.

And I sherry glasses.

I do not care for sherry I used to use for castor-oil.

You mean licorice.

He is so fond of coffee.

Let me tell you about kissing. We saw a piece of mistletoe. We exchanged a pillow. We murmured training and we were asleep.

This is what happened Saturday.

Another day we said sour grass it grows in fields. So do daisies and green flowers.

I have never noticed green flowers.

Lifting belly is my joy.

What did I tell Caesars.

That I recognised them.

It is the custom to answer swimming.

Catch a call.

Does the moonlight make any difference to you.

Lifting belly yes Miss.

I can lean upon a pencil.

Lifting belly yes address me.

I address you.

Lifting belly magnetically.

Did you make a mistake.

Wave to me.

Lifting belly permanently.

What did the Caesars.

What did they all say.

They said that they were not deceived.

Lifting belly such a good example. And is so readily watchful.

What do you think of watches.

Collect lobsters.

And sweetbreads.
And a melon.
And salad.
Do not have a term.
You mean what do you call it.
Yes sir.
Sing to me.
Lifting belly is neglected.
The Caesar.
Oh yes the Caesar.
Oh yes the Caesar.
Lifting belly pencils to me.
And pens.
Lifting belly and the intention.
I particularly like what I know.
Lifting belly sublimely.
We made a fire this evening.
Cooking is cheap.
I do not care for Ethel.
That's a very good one. I say that's a very good one.
Yes and we think.
A rhyme, I understand nectarine. I also understand egg.
A special case you are.
Lifting belly and Caesar.
Did I explain it.
Have I explained it to you.
Have I explained it to you in season. Have I perplexed you. You have not perplexed me nor mixed me. You have addressed me as Caesar. This is the answer that I expected. When I said do not mention

any words I meant no indifference. I meant do your duty and do not forget that I establish myself.

You establish yourself.

When this you see believe me.

Lifting belly etcetera.

Lifting belly and a hand. A hand is black and not by toil. I do not like fat resemblances. There are none such.

Lifting belly and kind.

This is the pencil for me.

Lifting belly squeezes.

Remember what I said about a rhyme.

Don't call it again.

Say white spots.

Do not mention disappointment in cups.

Oh you are so sweet.

Lifting belly believe me.

Believe it is for pleasure that I do it.

Not foreign pleasure.

Oh no.

My pleasure in Susie.

Lifting belly so kind.

So kindly.

Lifting belly gratuitously.

Lifting belly increase.

Do this to me.

Lifting belly famously.

When did I say I thought it.

When you heard it.

Oh yes.

Bright eyes I make you ties.

No mockings.

This is to say I knit woolen stockings for you.
And I understand it and I am very grateful.
Making a spectacle.
Drinking prepared water.
Laughing together.
Asking lifting belly to be particular.
Lifting belly is so kind.
She was like that.
Star spangled banner, story of Savannah.
She left because she was going to have the child
with her.
Lifting belly don't think of it.
Believe me in truth and marriage.
Believe that I use the best paper that I can get.
Do you believe me.
Lifting belly is not an invitation.
Call me semblances.
I call you a cab sir.
That's the way she tells it.
Lifting belly is so accurate.
I congratulate you in being respectable and re-
spectably married.
Call me Helen.
Not at all.
You may call me Helen.
That's what we said.
Lifting belly with firmness and pride.
Lifting belly with industry beside.
Heated heated with cold.
Some people are heated with linen.
Lifting belly comes extra.
This is a picture of lifting belly having a cow.
Oh yes you can say it of me.

When this you see remember me.
Lifting belly says pardon.
Pardon for what.
For having made a mistake.
Can you imagine what I say.
I say impossible.
Lifting belly is recognised.
Lifting belly presumably.
Do we run together.
I say do we run together.
I do not like stubbornness.
Come and sing.
Lifting belly.
I sing lifting belly.
I say lifting belly and then I say lifting belly and
Caesars. I say lifting belly gently and Caesars gently.
I say lifting belly again and Caesars again. I say
lifting belly and I say Caesars and I say lifting belly
Caesars and cow come out. I say lifting belly and
Caesars and cow come out.
Can you read my print.
Lifting belly say can you see the Caesars. I can
see what I kiss.
Of course you can.
Lifting belly high.
That is what I adore always more and more.
Come out cow.
Little connections.
Yes oh yes cow come out.
Lifting belly unerringly.
A wonderful book.
Baby my baby I backhand for thee.
She is a sweet baby and well baby and me.

This is the way I see it.
Lifting belly can you say it.
Lifting belly persuade me.
Lifting belly persuade me.
You'll find it a very easy to sing to me.
What can you say.
Lifting belly set.
I can not pass a door.
You mean odor.
I smell sweetly.
So do you.
Lifting belly plainly.
Can you sing.
Can you sing for me.
Lifting belly settled.
Can you excuse money.
Lifting belly has a dress.
Lifting belly in a mess.
Lifting belly in order.
Complain I don't complain.
She is my sweetheart.
Why doesn't she resemble an other.
This I cannot say here.
Full of love and echoes. Lifting belly is full of
love.
Can you.
Can you can you.
Can you buy a Ford.
Did you expect that.
Lifting belly hungrily.
Not lonesomely.
But enthusiastically.
Lifting belly altogether.

Were you wise.
Were you wise to do so.
Can you say winking.
Can you say Francis Ferdinand has gone to the West.
Can you neglect me.
Can you establish the clock.
Yes I can when I am good.
Lifting belly precariously.
Lifting belly is noted.
Are you noted with me.
Come to sing and sit.
This is not the time for discussion.
A splendid table little table.
A splendid little table.
Can you be fortunate.
Yes sir.
What is a man.
What is a woman.
What is a bird.
Lifting belly must please me.
Yes can you think so.
Lifting belly cherished and flattered.
Lifting belly naturally.
Can you extract.
Can you be through so quickly.
No I cannot get through so quickly.
Are you afraid of Negro sculpture.
I have my feelings.
Lifting belly is so exact.
Lifting belly is favored by me.
Lifting belly cautiously.
I lift it in place of the music.

You mean it is the same.
I mean everything.
Can you not whistle.
Call me for that.
And sing.
I sing too.
Lifting belly counts.
My idea is.
Yes I know what your idea is.
Lifting belly knows all about the wind.
Yes indeed Miss.
Yes indeed.
Can you suspect me.
We are glad that we do not deceive.
Lifting belly regular.
Lifted belly behind.
Candidly.
Can you say that there is a mistake.
In the wash.
No in respect to the woman.
Can you say we meant to send her away.
Lifting belly is so orderly.
She makes no mistake.
She does not indeed.
Lifting belly heroically.
Can you think of that.
Can you guess what I mean.
Yes I can.
Lovely sweet.
Calville cow.
And that is it.
Lifting belly resignedly.
Now you laugh.

Lifting belly for me.
When this you see remember me.
Can you be sweet.
You are.
We are so likely.
We are so likely to be sweet.
Lifting belly handy.
Can you mention lifting belly. I can.
Yes indeed I know what I say.
Do you.
Lifting belly is so much.
Lifting belly grandly.
You can be sweet.
We see it.
We are tall.
We are wellbred.
We can say we do like what we have.
Lifting belly is more.
I am more than ever inclined to how do you do.
That's the way to wish it.
Lifting belly is so good.
That is natural.
Lifting belly exactly.
Calville cow is all to me.
Don't excite me.
Lifting belly exactly.
That's respectable.
Lifting belly is all to me.
Pretty Caesars yes they do.
Can you spell mixing.
I hear you.
How do you do.
Can you tell me about imposing.

When are you careful to speak.
Lifting belly categorically.
Think of it.
Lifting belly in the mind.
The Honorable Graham Murray.
My honorable Graham Murray.
What can you say.
I can say that I find it most useful and very
warm, yet light.
Lifting belly astonishingly.
Can you mention her brother.
Yes.
Her father.
Yes.
A married couple.
Yes.
Lifting belly names it.
Look at that.
Yes that's what I said.
I put down something on lifting belly.
Humph.
Lifting belly bells.
Can you think of singing. In the little while in
which I say stop it you are not spoiled.
Can you be spoiled. I do not think so.
I think not.
I think everything of you.
Lifting belly is rich.
Chickens are rich.
I cannot disguise nice.
Don't you need to.
I think not.
Lifting belly exactly.

Why can lifting belly please me.

Lifting belly can please me because it is an occupation I enjoy.

Rose is a rose is a rose is a rose.

In print on top.

What can you do.

I can answer my question.

Very well answer this.

Who is Mr. Mc Bride.

In the way of laughing.

Lifting belly is an intention.

You are sure you know the meaning of any word.

Leave me to see.

Pink.

My pink.

Hear me to-day.

It is after noon.

I mean that literally.

It is after noon.

Little lifting belly is a quotation.

Frankly what do you say to me.

I say that I need protection.

You shall have it.

After that what do you wish.

I want you to mean a great deal to me.

Exactly.

And then.

And then blandishment.

We can see that very clearly.

Lifting belly is perfect.

Do you stretch farther.

Come eat it.

What did I say.

To whom.

Calville or a cow.

We were in a fashion deceived in Calville but not in a cow.

I understand when they say they mean something by it.

Lifting belly grandly.

Lifting belly sufficiently.

Come and be awake.

Certainly this morning.

Lifting belly very much.

I do not feel that I will be deceived.

Lifting belly fairly.

You mean follow.

I mean I follow.

Need you wish me to say lifting belly is recognised. No it is not necessary lifting belly is not peculiar. It is recognised. Can you recognise it. In a flash.

Thank you for me.

Can you excuse any one for loving its dearest. I said from. That is eaten.

Can you excuse any one from loving its dearest.

No I cannot.

A special fabric.

Can you begin a new thing.

Can I begin.

We have a dress.

You have a dress.

A dress by him.

Feel me.

I feel you.

Then it is fair to me.

Let me sing.

Certainly.

And you too Miss Polly.

What can you say.

I can say that there is no need of regretting a ball.

Mount Fatty.

That is a tremendous way.

Leave me to sing about it to-day.

And then there was a cake. Please give it to me. She did.

When can there be glasses. We are so pleased with it.

Go on to-morrow.

He cannot understand women. I can.

Believe me in this way.

I can understand the woman.

Lifting belly carelessly. I do not lift baby carelessly.

Lifting belly because there is no mistake. I planned to flourish. Of course you do.

Lifting belly is exacting. You mean exact. I mean exacting. Lifting belly is exacting.

Can you say see me.

Lifting belly is exciting.

Can you explain a mistake.

There is no mistake.

You have mentioned the flour.

Lifting belly is full of charm.

They are very nice candles.

Lifting belly is resourceful.

What can lifting belly say.

Oh yes I was not mistaken. Were not you indeed.

Lifting belly lifting belly lifting belly oh then lifting belly.

Can you make an expression. Thanks for the cigarette. How pretty.

How fast. What. How fast the cow comes out.

Lifting belly a permanent caress.

Lifting belly bored.

You don't say so.

Lifting belly now.

Cow.

Lifting belly exactly.

I have often been pleased with this thing.

Lifting belly is necessarily venturesome.

You mean by that that you are collected. I hope I am.

What is an evening dress. What is a cape. What is a suit. What is a fur collar.

Lifting belly needs to speak.

Land Rising next time.

Lifting belly has no choice.

Lifting belly seems to me to be remarkably kind.

Can you hear me witness that I was wolfish. I can. And that I do not interfere with you. No I cannot countenance you here. Countenance what do you mean by that. I mean that it is a pleasure to prepare you. Thank you my dear.

Lifting belly is so kind.

Can you recollect this for me.

Lifting belly naturally.

Can you believe the truth.

Fredericks or Frederica.

Can you give me permission.

The Loves.

I never forget the Caesars.
Or the dears.
Lifting belly casually.
Where the head gets thin.
Lifting belly never mind.
You do please me.
Lifting belly restless.
Not at all.
Lifting belly there.
Expand my chest endlessly.
You did not do so.
Lifting belly is loved.
You know I am always ready to please you.
Lifting belly in a breath.
Lifting belly.
You do speak kindly.
We speak very kindly.
Lifting belly is so bold.

III
Lifting belly in here.
Able to state whimsies.
Can you recollect mistakes.
I hope not.
Bless you.
Lifting belly the best and only seat.
Lifting belly the reminder of present duties.
Lifting belly the charm.
Lifting belly is easy to me.
Lifting belly naturally.
Of course you lift belly naturally.
I lift belly naturally together.
Lifting belly answers.

Can you think for me.

I can.

Lifting belly endears me.

Lifting belly cleanly. With a wood fire. With a good fire.

Say how do you do to the lady. Which lady. The jew lady. How do you do. She is my wife.

Can you accuse lifting belly of extras.

Salmon is salmon. Smoked and the most nourishing.

Pink salmon is my favorite color.

To be sure.

We are so necessary.

Can you wish for me.

I never mention it.

You need not resemble me.

But you do.

Of course you do.

That is very well said.

And meant.

And explained.

I explain too much.

And then I say.

She knows everything.

And she does.

Lifting belly beneficently.

I can go on with lifting belly forever. And you do.

I said it first. Lifting belly to engage. And then wishes. I wish to be whimsied. I do that.

A worldly system.

A humorous example.

Lindo see me.

Whimsy see me.

See me.

Lifting belly exaggerates. Lifting belly is reproach-ful.

Oh can you see.

Yes sir.

Lifting belly mentions the bee.

Can you imagine the noise.

Can you whisper to me.

Lifting belly pronouncedly.

Can you imagine me thinking lifting belly.

Safety first.

That's the trimming.

I hear her snore

On through the door.

I can say that it is my delight.

Lifting belly fairly well.

Lifting belly visibly.

Yes I say visibly.

Lifting belly behind me.

The room is so pretty and clean.

Do you know the rest.

Yes I know the rest.

She knows the rest and will do it.

Lifting belly in eclipse.

There is no such moon for me.

Eclipse indeed can lifting belly be methodical.

In lifting belly yes.

In lifting belly yes.

Can you think of me.

I can and do.

Lifting belly encourages plenty.

Do not speak of San Francisco he is a saint.

Lifting belly shines.

Lifting belly nattily.
Lifting belly to fly.
Not to-day.
Motor.
Lifting belly for wind.
We do not like wind.
We do not mind snow.
Lifting belly partially.
Can you spell for me.
Spell bottle.
Lifting belly remarks.
Can we have the hill.
Of course we can have the hill.
Lifting belly patiently.
Can you see me rise.
Lifting belly says she can.
Lifting belly soundly.
Here is a bun for my bunny.
Every little bun is of honey.
On the little bun is my oney.
My little bun is so funny.
Sweet little bun for my money.
Dear little but I'm her sunny.
Sweet little bun dear little bun good little bun for
my bunny.
Lifting belly merry Christmas.
Lifting belly has wishes.
And then we please her.
What is the name of that pin.
Not a hat pin.
We use elastic.
As garters.
We are never blamed.

Thank you and see me.
How can I swim.
By not being surprised.
Lifting belly is so kind.
Lifting belly is harmonious.
Can you smile to me.
Lifting belly is prepared.
Can you imagine what I say.
Lifting belly can.
To be remarkable.
To be remarkably so.
Lifting belly and emergencies.
Lifting belly in reading.
Can you say effectiveness.
Lifting belly in reserve.
Lifting belly marches.
There is no song.
Lifting belly marry.
Lifting belly can see the condition.
How do you spell Lindo.
Not to displease.
The dears.
When can I.
When can I.
To-morrow if you like.
Thank you so much.
See you.
We were pleased to receive notes.
In there.
To there.
Can you see spelling.
Anybody can see lines.
Lifting belly is arrogant.

Not with oranges.
Lifting belly inclines me.
To see clearly.
Lifting belly is for me.
I can say truthfully never better.
Believe me lifting belly is not nervous.
Lifting belly is a miracle.
I am with her.
Lifting belly to me.
Very nicely done.
Poetry is very nicely done.
Can you say pleasure.
I can easily say please me.
You do.
Lifting belly is precious.
Then you can sing.
We do not encourage a nightingale.
Do you really mean that.
We literally do.
Then it is an intention.
Not the smell.
Lifting baby is a chance.
Certainly sir.
I please myself.
Can we convince Morlet.
We can.
Then see the way.
We can have a pleasant ford.
And we do.
We will.
See my baby cheerily.
I am celebrated by the lady.
Indeed you are.

I can rhyme.
In English.
In loving.
In preparing.
Do not be rough.
I can sustain conversation.
Do you like a title for you.
Do you like a title.
Do you like my title.
Can you agree.
We do.
In that way have candles.
And dirt.
Not dirt.
There are two Caesars and there are four Caesars.
Caesars do their duty.
I never make a mistake.
We will be very happy and boastful and we will
celebrate Sunday.
How do you like your Aunt Pauline.
She is worthy of a queen.
Will she go as we do dream.
She will do satisfactorily.
And so will we.
Thank you so much.
Smiling to me.
Then we can see him.
Yes we can.
Can we always go.
I think so.
You will be secure.
We are secure.
Then we see.

We see the way.
This is very good for me.
In this way we play.
Then we are pleasing.
We are pleasing to him.
We have gone together.
We are in our Ford.
Please me please me.
We go then.
We go when.
In a minute.
Next week.
Yes indeed oh yes indeed.
I can tell you she is charming in a coat.
Yes and we are full of her praises.
Yes indeed.
This is the way to worry. Not it.
Can you smile.
Yes indeed oh yes indeed.
And so can I.
Can we think.
Wrist leading.
Wrist leading.
A kind of exercise.
A brilliant station.
Do you remember its name.
Yes Morlet.
Can you say wishes.
I can.
Winning baby.
Theoretically and practically.
Can we explain a season.
We can when we are right.

Two is too many.
To be right.
One is right and so we mount and have what we want.
We will remember.
Can you mix birthdays.
Certainly I can.
Then do so.
I do so.
Do I remember to write.
Can he paint.
Not after he has driven a car.
I can write.
There you are.
Lifting belly with me.
You inquire.
What you do then.
Pushing.
Thank you so much.
And lend a hand.
What is lifting belly now.
My baby.
Always sincerely.
Lifting belly says it there.
Thank you for the cream.
Lifting belly tenderly.
A remarkable piece of intuition.
I have forgotten all about it.
Have you forgotten all about it.
Little nature which is mine.
Fairy ham
Is a clam.
Of chowder

Kiss him Louder.
Can you be especially proud of me.
Lifting belly a queen.
In that way I can think.
Thank you so much.
I have,
Lifting belly for me.
I can not forget the name.
Lifting belly for me.
Lifting belly again.
Can you be proud of me.
I am.
Then we say it.
In miracles.
Can we say it and then sing. You mean drive.
I mean to drive.
We are full of pride.
Lifting belly is proud.
Lifting belly my queen.
Lifting belly happy.
Lifting belly see.
Lifting belly.
Lifting belly address.
Little washers.
Lifting belly how do you do.
Lifting belly is famous for recipes.
You mean Genevieve.
I mean I never ask for potatoes.
But you liked them then.
And now.
Now we know about water.
Lifting belly is a miracle.
And the Caesars.

The Caesars are docile.
Not more docile than is right.
No beautifully right.
And in relation to a cow.
And in relation to a cow.
Do believe me when I incline.
You mean obey.
I mean obey.
Obey me.
Husband obey your wife.
Lifting belly is so dear.
To me.
Lifting belly is smooth,
Tell lifting belly about matches.
Matches can be struck with the thumb.
Not by us.
No indeed.
What is it I say about letters.
Twenty six.
And counted.
And counted deliberately.
This is not as difficult as it seems.
Lifting belly is so strange
And quick.
Lifting belly in a minute.
Lifting belly in a minute now.
In a minute.
Not to-day.
No not to-day.
Can you swim.
Lifting belly can perform aquatics.
Lifting belly is astonishing.
Lifting belly for me.

Come together.
Lifting belly near.
I credit you with repetition.
Believe me I will not say it.
And retirement.
I celebrate something.
Do you.
Lifting belly extraordinarily in haste.
I am so sorry I said it.
Lifting belly is a credit. Do you care about poetry.
Lifting belly in spots.
Do you like ink.
Better than butter.
Better than anything.
Any letter is an alphabet.
When this you see you will kiss me.
Lifting belly is so generous.
Shoes.
Servant.
And Florence.
Then we can sing.
We do among.
I like among.
Lifting belly keeps.
Thank you in lifting belly.
Can you wonder that they don't make preserves.
We ask the question and they answer you give us
help.
Lifting belly is so successful.
Is she indeed.
I wish you would not be disobliging.
In that way I am.
But in giving.

In giving you always win.
You mean in effect.
I mean in essence.
Thank you so much we are so much obliged.
This may be a case
Have no fear.
Then we can be indeed.
You are and you must.
Thank you so much.
In kindness you excel.
You have obliged me too.
I have done what is necessary.
Then can I say thank you may I say thank you
very much.
Thank you again.
Because lifting belly is about baby.
Three eggs in lifting belly.
Éclair.
Think of it.
Think of that.
We think of that.
We produce music.
And in sleeping.
Noises.
Can that be she.
Lifting belly is so kind
Darling wifie is so good.
Little husband would.
Be as good.
If he could.
This was said.
Now we know how to differ.
From that.

Certainly.
Now we say.
Little hubbie is good.
Every Day.
She did want a photograph.
Lifting belly changed her mind.
Lifting belly changed her mind.
Do I look fat.
Do I look fat and thin.
Blue eyes and windows.
You mean Vera.
Lifting belly can guess.
Quickly.
Lifting belly is so pleased.
Lifting belly seeks pleasure.
And she finds it altogether.
Lifting belly is my love.
Can you say meritorious.
Yes camellia.
Why do you complain.
Postal cards.
And then.
The Louvre.
After that.
After that Francine.
You don't mean by that name.
What is Spain.
Listen lightly.
But you do.
Don't tell me what you call me.
But he is pleased.
But he is pleased.
That is the way it sounds.

In the morning.
By that bright light.
Will you exchange purses.
You know I like to please you.
Lifting belly is so kind.
Then sign.
I sign the bulletin.
Do the boys remember that nicely
To-morrow we go there.
And the photographs
The photographs will come.
When
You will see.
Will it please me.
Not suddenly
But soon
Very soon.
But you will hear first.
That will take some time.
Not very long.
What do you mean by long.
A few days.
How few days.
One or two days.
Thank you for saying so.
Thank you so much.
Lifting belly waits splendidly.
For essence.
For essence too.
Can you assure me.
I can and do.
Very well it will come.
And I will be happy.

You are happy.
And I will be
You always will be.
Lifting belly sings nicely.
Not nervously.
No not nervously.
Nicely and forcefully.
Lifting belly is so sweet.
Can you say you say.
In this thought.
I do think lifting belly.
Little love lifting
Little love light.
Little love heavy.
Lifting belly tight.
Thank you.
Can you turn over.
Rapidly.
Lifting belly so meaningly.
Yes indeed the dog.
He watches.
The little boys.
They whistle on their legs,
Little boys have meadows,
Then they are well.
Very well.
Please be the man.
I am the man.
Lifting belly praises.
And she gives
Health.
And fragrance.
And words.

Lifting belly is in bed.
And the bed has been made comfortable.
Lifting belly knows this.
Spain and torn
Whistling.
Can she whistle to me.
Lifting belly in a flash.
You know the word.
Strawberries grown in Perpignan are not particularly good.
These are inferior kinds.
Kind are a kind.
Lifting belly is sugar.
Lifting belly to me.
In this way I can see.
What
Lifting belly dictate.
Daisy dear.
Lifting belly
Lifting belly carelessly.
I didn't.
I see why you are careful
Can you stick a stick. In what In the carpet.
Can you be careful of the corner.
Mrs. the Mrs. indeed yes.
Lifting belly is charming.
Often to-morrow
I'll try again.
This time I will sin
Not by a prophecy.
That is the truth.
Very well.
When will they change.

They have changed.
Then they are coming.
Yes.
Soon.
On the way.
I like the smell of gloves.
Lifting belly has money.
Do you mean cuckoo.
A funny noise.
In the meantime there was lots of singing.
And then and then.
We have a new game
Can you fill it.
Alone.
And is it good
And useful
And has it a name
Lifting belly can change to filling petunia.
But not the same.
It is not the same.
It is the same.
Lifting belly.
So high.
And aiming.
Exactly.
And making
A cow
Come out.
Indeed I was not mistaken.
Come do not have a cow.
He has.
Well then.
Dear Daisy.

She is a dish.
A dish of good.
Perfect.
Pleasure.
In the way of dishes.
Willy.
And Milly.
In words.
So loud.
Lifting belly the dear.
Protection.
Protection
Protection
Speculation
Protection
Protection.
Can the furniture shine.
Ask me.
What is my answer.
Beautifully.
Is there a way of being careful
Of what.
Of the South.
By going to it.
We will go.
For them.
For them again.
And is there any likelihood of butter.
We do not need butter.
Lifting belly enormously and with song.
Can you sing about a cow.
Yes.
And about signs.

Yes.
And also about Aunt Pauline.
Yes.
Can you sing at your work.
Yes.
In the meantime listen to Miss Cheatham.
In the midst of writing.
In the midst of writing there is merriment.

A few of the publications of
THE NAIAD PRESS, INC.
P.O. Box 10543 ● Tallahassee, Florida 32302
Phone (904) 539-5965
Mail orders welcome. Please include 15% postage.

THE BEVERLY MALIBU by Katherine V. Forrest. 288 pp. A
Kate Delafield Mystery. 3rd in a series.   ISBN 0-941483-47-9 $16.95

THERE'S SOMETHING I'VE BEEN MEANING TO TELL
YOU Ed. by Loralee MacPike. 288 pp. Gay men and lesbians
coming out to their children.   ISBN 0-941483-44-4   9.95
    ISBN 0-941483-54-1   16.95

LIFTING BELLY by Gertrude Stein. Ed. by Rebecca Mark. 104
pp. Erotic poetry.   ISBN 0-941483-51-7   8.95
    ISBN 0-941483-53-3   14.95

ROSE PENSKI by Roz Perry. 192 pp. Adult lovers in a long-term
relationship.   ISBN 0-941483-37-1   8.95

AFTER THE FIRE by Jane Rule. 256 pp. Warm, human novel
by this incomparable author.   ISBN 0-941483-45-2   8.95

SUE SLATE, PRIVATE EYE by Lee Lynch. 176 pp. The gay
folk of Peacock Alley are *all* cats.   ISBN 0-941483-52-5   8.95

CHRIS by Randy Salem. 224 pp. Golden oldie. Handsome Chris
and her adventures.   ISBN 0-941483-42-8   8.95

THREE WOMEN by March Hastings. 232 pp. Golden oldie. A
triangle among wealthy sophisticates.   ISBN 0-941483-43-6   8.95

RICE AND BEANS by Valeria Taylor. 232 pp. Love and
romance on poverty row.   ISBN 0-941483-41-X   8.95

PLEASURES by Robbi Sommers. 204 pp. Unprecedented
eroticism.   ISBN 0-941483-49-5   8.95

EDGEWISE by Camarin Grae. 372 pp. Spellbinding
adventure.   ISBN 0-941483-19-3   9.95

FATAL REUNION by Claire McNab. 216 pp. 2nd Det. Inspec.
Carol Ashton mystery.   ISBN 0-941483-40-1   8.95

KEEP TO ME STRANGER by Sarah Aldridge. 372 pp. Romance
set in a department store dynasty.   ISBN 0-941483-38-X   9.95

HEARTSCAPE by Sue Gambill. 204 pp. American lesbian in
Portugal.   ISBN 0-941483-33-9   8.95

IN THE BLOOD by Lauren Wright Douglas. 252 pp. Lesbian
science fiction adventure fantasy   ISBN 0-941483-22-3   8.95

THE BEE'S KISS by Shirley Verel. 216 pp. Delicate, delicious
romance.   ISBN 0-941483-36-3   8.95

RAGING MOTHER MOUNTAIN by Pat Emmerson. 264 pp.
Furosa Firechild's adventures in Wonderland. ISBN 0-941483-35-5   8.95

IN EVERY PORT by Karin Kallmaker. 228 pp. Jessica's sexy,
adventuresome travels. ISBN 0-941483-37-7   8.95

OF LOVE AND GLORY by Evelyn Kennedy. 192 pp. Exciting
WWII romance. ISBN 0-941483-32-0   8.95

CLICKING STONES by Nancy Tyler Glenn. 288 pp. Love
transcending time. ISBN 0-941483-31-2   8.95

SURVIVING SISTERS by Gail Pass. 252 pp. Powerful love
story. ISBN 0-941483-16-9   8.95

SOUTH OF THE LINE by Catherine Ennis. 216 pp. Civil War
adventure. ISBN 0-941483-29-0   8.95

WOMAN PLUS WOMAN by Dolores Klaich. 300 pp. Supurb
Lesbian overview. ISBN 0-941483-28-2   9.95

SLOW DANCING AT MISS POLLY'S by Sheila Ortiz Taylor.
96 pp. Lesbian Poetry ISBN 0-941483-30-4   7.95

DOUBLE DAUGHTER by Vicki P. McConnell. 216 pp. A Nyla
Wade Mystery, third in the series. ISBN 0-941483-26-6   8.95

HEAVY GILT by Delores Klaich. 192 pp. Lesbian detective/
disappearing homophobes/upper class gay society.
ISBN 0-941483-25-8   8.95

THE FINER GRAIN by Denise Ohio. 216 pp. Brilliant young
college lesbian novel. ISBN 0-941483-11-8   8.95

THE AMAZON TRAIL by Lee Lynch. 216 pp. Life, travel & lore
of famous lesbian author. ISBN 0-941483-27-4   8.95

HIGH CONTRAST by Jessie Lattimore. 264 pp. Women of the
Crystal Palace. ISBN 0-941483-17-7   8.95

OCTOBER OBSESSION by Meredith More. Josie's rich, secret
Lesbian life. ISBN 0-941483-18-5   8.95

LESBIAN CROSSROADS by Ruth Baetz. 276 pp. Contemporary
Lesbian lives. ISBN 0-941483-21-5   9.95

BEFORE STONEWALL: THE MAKING OF A GAY AND
LESBIAN COMMUNITY by Andrea Weiss & Greta Schiller.
96 pp., 25 illus. ISBN 0-941483-20-7   7.95

WE WALK THE BACK OF THE TIGER by Patricia A. Murphy.
192 pp. Romantic Lesbian novel/beginning women's movement.
ISBN 0-941483-13-4   8.95

SUNDAY'S CHILD by Joyce Bright. 216 pp. Lesbian athletics, at
last the novel about sports. ISBN 0-941483-12-6   8.95

OSTEN'S BAY by Zenobia N. Vole. 204 pp. Sizzling adventure
romance set on Bonaire. ISBN 0-941483-15-0   8.95

LESSONS IN MURDER by Claire McNab. 216 pp. 1st Det. Inspec.
Carol Ashton mystery — erotic tension!. ISBN 0-941483-14-2   8.95

YELLOWTHROAT by Penny Hayes. 240 pp. Margarita, bandit,
kidnaps Julia.   ISBN 0-941483-10-X   8.95

SAPPHISTRY: THE BOOK OF LESBIAN SEXUALITY by
Pat Califia. 3d edition, revised. 208 pp.   ISBN 0-941483-24-X   8.95

CHERISHED LOVE by Evelyn Kennedy. 192 pp. Erotic
Lesbian love story.   ISBN 0-941483-08-8   8.95

LAST SEPTEMBER by Helen R. Hull. 208 pp. Six stories & a
glorious novella.   ISBN 0-941483-09-6   8.95

THE SECRET IN THE BIRD by Camarin Grae. 312 pp. Striking,
psychological suspense novel.   ISBN 0-941483-05-3   8.95

TO THE LIGHTNING by Catherine Ennis. 208 pp. Romantic
Lesbian 'Robinson Crusoe' adventure.   ISBN 0-941483-06-1   8.95

THE OTHER SIDE OF VENUS by Shirley Verel. 224 pp.
Luminous, romantic love story.   ISBN 0-941483-07-X   8.95

DREAMS AND SWORDS by Katherine V. Forrest. 192 pp.
Romantic, erotic, imaginative stories.   ISBN 0-941483-03-7   8.95

MEMORY BOARD by Jane Rule. 336 pp. Memorable novel
about an aging Lesbian couple.   ISBN 0-941483-02-9   8.95

THE ALWAYS ANONYMOUS BEAST by Lauren Wright
Douglas. 224 pp. A Caitlin Reese mystery. First in a series.
                                         ISBN 0-941483-04-5   8.95

SEARCHING FOR SPRING by Patricia A. Murphy. 224 pp.
Novel about the recovery of love.   ISBN 0-941483-00-2   8.95

DUSTY'S QUEEN OF HEARTS DINER by Lee Lynch. 240 pp.
Romantic blue-collar novel.   ISBN 0-941483-01-0   8.95

PARENTS MATTER by Ann Muller. 240 pp. Parents'
relationships with Lesbian daughters and gay sons.
                                         ISBN 0-930044-91-6   9.95

THE PEARLS by Shelley Smith. 176 pp. Passion and fun in
the Caribbean sun.   ISBN 0-930044-93-2   7.95

MAGDALENA by Sarah Aldridge. 352 pp. Epic Lesbian novel
set on three continents.   ISBN 0-930044-99-1   8.95

THE BLACK AND WHITE OF IT by Ann Allen Shockley.
144 pp. Short stories.   ISBN 0-930044-96-7   7.95

SAY JESUS AND COME TO ME by Ann Allen Shockley. 288
pp. Contemporary romance.   ISBN 0-930044-98-3   8.95

LOVING HER by Ann Allen Shockley. 192 pp. Romantic love
story.   ISBN 0-930044-97-5   7.95

MURDER AT THE NIGHTWOOD BAR by Katherine V.
Forrest. 240 pp. A Kate Delafield mystery. Second in a series.
                                         ISBN 0-930044-92-4   8.95

ZOE'S BOOK by Gail Pass. 224 pp. Passionate, obsessive love
story.   ISBN 0-930044-95-9   7.95

WINGED DANCER by Camarin Grae. 228 pp. Erotic Lesbian
adventure story.   ISBN 0-930044-88-6   8.95

PAZ by Camarin Grae. 336 pp. Romantic Lesbian adventurer
with the power to change the world.   ISBN 0-930044-89-4   8.95

SOUL SNATCHER by Camarin Grae. 224 pp. A puzzle, an
adventure, a mystery — Lesbian romance.   ISBN 0-930044-90-8   8.95

THE LOVE OF GOOD WOMEN by Isabel Miller. 224 pp.
Long-awaited new novel by the author of the beloved *Patience
and Sarah.*   ISBN 0-930044-81-9   8.95

THE HOUSE AT PELHAM FALLS by Brenda Weathers. 240
pp. Suspenseful Lesbian ghost story.   ISBN 0-930044-79-7   7.95

HOME IN YOUR HANDS by Lee Lynch. 240 pp. More stories
from the author of *Old Dyke Tales.*   ISBN 0-930044-80-0   7.95

EACH HAND A MAP by Anita Skeen. 112 pp. Real-life poems
that touch us all.   ISBN 0-930044-82-7   6.95

SURPLUS by Sylvia Stevenson. 342 pp. A classic early Lesbian
novel.   ISBN 0-930044-78-9   7.95

PEMBROKE PARK by Michelle Martin. 256 pp. Derring-do
and daring romance in Regency England.   ISBN 0-930044-77-0   7.95

THE LONG TRAIL by Penny Hayes. 248 pp. Vivid adventures
of two women in love in the old west.   ISBN 0-930044-76-2   8.95

HORIZON OF THE HEART by Shelley Smith. 192 pp. Hot
romance in summertime New England.   ISBN 0-930044-75-4   7.95

AN EMERGENCE OF GREEN by Katherine V. Forrest. 288
pp. Powerful novel of sexual discovery.   ISBN 0-930044-69-X   8.95

THE LESBIAN PERIODICALS INDEX edited by Claire
Potter. 432 pp. Author & subject index.   ISBN 0-930044-74-6   29.95

DESERT OF THE HEART by Jane Rule. 224 pp. A classic;
basis for the movie *Desert Hearts.*   ISBN 0-930044-73-8   7.95

SPRING FORWARD/FALL BACK by Sheila Ortiz Taylor.
288 pp. Literary novel of timeless love.   ISBN 0-930044-70-3   7.95

FOR KEEPS by Elisabeth Nonas. 144 pp. Contemporary novel
about losing and finding love.   ISBN 0-930044-71-1   7.95

TORCHLIGHT TO VALHALLA by Gale Wilhelm. 128 pp.
Classic novel by a great Lesbian writer.   ISBN 0-930044-68-1   7.95

LESBIAN NUNS: BREAKING SILENCE edited by Rosemary
Curb and Nancy Manahan. 432 pp. Unprecedented autobiographies
of religious life.   ISBN 0-930044-62-2   9.95

THE SWASHBUCKLER by Lee Lynch. 288 pp. Colorful novel
set in Greenwich Village in the sixties.   ISBN 0-930044-66-5   8.95

TO THE CLEVELAND STATION by Carol Anne Douglas. 192 pp. Interracial Lesbian love story. ISBN 0-930044-27-4   6.95

THE NESTING PLACE by Sarah Aldridge. 224 pp. A three-woman triangle—love conquers all! ISBN 0-930044-26-6   7.95

THIS IS NOT FOR YOU by Jane Rule. 284 pp. A letter to a beloved is also an intricate novel. ISBN 0-930044-25-8   8.95

FAULTLINE by Sheila Ortiz Taylor. 140 pp. Warm, funny, literate story of a startling family. ISBN 0-930044-24-X   6.95

THE LESBIAN IN LITERATURE by Barbara Grier. 3d ed. Foreword by Maida Tilchen. 240 pp. Comprehensive bibliography. Literary ratings; rare photos. ISBN 0-930044-23-1   7.95

ANNA'S COUNTRY by Elizabeth Lang. 208 pp. A woman finds her Lesbian identity. ISBN 0-930044-19-3   6.95

PRISM by Valerie Taylor. 158 pp. A love affair between two women in their sixties. ISBN 0-930044-18-5   6.95

BLACK LESBIANS: AN ANNOTATED BIBLIOGRAPHY compiled by J. R. Roberts. Foreword by Barbara Smith. 112 pp. Award-winning bibliography. ISBN 0-930044-21-5   5.95

THE MARQUISE AND THE NOVICE by Victoria Ramstetter. 108 pp. A Lesbian Gothic novel. ISBN 0-930044-16-9   6.95

OUTLANDER by Jane Rule. 207 pp. Short stories and essays by one of our finest writers. ISBN 0-930044-17-7   8.95

ALL TRUE LOVERS by Sarah Aldridge. 292 pp. Romantic novel set in the 1930s and 1940s. ISBN 0-930044-10-X   7.95

A WOMAN APPEARED TO ME by Renee Vivien. 65 pp. A classic; translated by Jeannette H. Foster. ISBN 0-930044-06-1   5.00

CYTHEREA'S BREATH by Sarah Aldridge. 240 pp. Romantic novel about women's entrance into medicine. ISBN 0-930044-02-9   6.95

TOTTIE by Sarah Aldridge. 181 pp. Lesbian romance in the turmoil of the sixties. ISBN 0-930044-01-0   6.95

THE LATECOMER by Sarah Aldridge. 107 pp. A delicate love story. ISBN 0-930044-00-2   6.95

ODD GIRL OUT by Ann Bannon. ISBN 0-930044-83-5   5.95

I AM A WOMAN by Ann Bannon. ISBN 0-930044-84-3   5.95

WOMEN IN THE SHADOWS by Ann Bannon. ISBN 0-930044-85-1   5.95

JOURNEY TO A WOMAN by Ann Bannon. ISBN 0-930044-86-X   5.95

BEEBO BRINKER by Ann Bannon. ISBN 0-930044-87-8   5.95
Legendary novels written in the fifties and sixties, set in the gay mecca of Greenwich Village.

VOLUTE BOOKS

JOURNEY TO FULFILLMENT	Early classics by Valerie	3.95
A WORLD WITHOUT MEN	Taylor: The Erika Frohmann	3.95
RETURN TO LESBOS	series.	3.95

These are just a few of the many Naiad Press titles — we are the oldest and largest lesbian/feminist publishing company in the world. Please request a complete catalog. We offer personal service; we encourage and welcome direct mail orders from individuals who have limited access to bookstores carrying our publications.